More Advance Praise For *Uncle Feygele*

Switching back and forth from English to Yiddish, Yermiyahu Ahron Taub's poetry is at once socially engaged and sexy. The collection as a whole, which includes poems in honor of the social democrat Rosa Luxemburg and the Hebrew poet Rahel, and the "unnamed and unremembered," is beautifully crafted. His poems on men ... sizzling.

David Shneer
Author of *Through Soviet Jewish Eyes: Photography, War, and the Holocaust*

Who is this Uncle Feygele, this little bird, who moves and loves though the ages? Yermiyahu Ahron Taub has created a voice of longing in a persona embodying the female, male and child caught being both outsider and insider—a gay Orthodox Jew. He is a man in a community of faith, family, place and history. Taub writes in a lyrical language strikingly sensual, rolling in long lines that seem to wash over the edge of the page and splash in limpid beauty crossing all borders civilization places on human interaction. Feygele, a derogatory term for Jewish homosexual, becomes a persona incorporating all the same wishes, fears, and history as "straights." We are the same—gay, lesbian, straight, bi or trans—all deserving respect not oppression.

Eve Rifkah
Author of *Dear Suzanne* and *Outcasts*

Uncle Feygele

poems by

Yermiyahu Ahron Taub

Plain View Press
P.O. 42255
Austin, TX 78704

plainviewpress.net
pk@plainviewpress.net
512-441-2452

ISBN: 978-1-935514-86-2
Library of Congress Control Number: 2010942827

Cover art "Hasid Mask with Green Background"
        by Aaron Mayer Frankel.
Cover design by Susan Bright.

For Pearl Gluck

פּערעלען

א״ר אלעזר כל אדם שאין לו אשה אינו אדם שנאמר זכר ונקבה בראם ויקרא את שמם אדם.

— מסכת יבמות, סג.

Rabbi Elazar said that a man without a wife is not a man, as it is stated male and female He created them, and He called them by the name of man.

—Babylonian Talmud, Tractate Yevamot 63a

הקהל את העם האנשים והנשים והטף וגרך אשר בשעריך למען ישמעו ולמען ילמדו ויראו את יהוה אלהיכם ושמרו לעשות את כל דברי התורה הזאת.

— דברים, לא:יב

Assemble the nation—the men, and the women, and the children, and the stranger within your gates—so that they may hear and that they may fear the Lord your God and take care to perform all the words of this Torah.

—Deuteronomy 31:12

Contents

III. Children   71

IV. Strangers At Your Gate   93

I

Women

A Map Of Commotion

In the surrounding region, the leaves of a world unfurled.
Between the mouths of trees, arrangements were made.
Food was delivered to the village crone without incident.
Come, young man, to the light in my fingers, she said.

A girl felt free to discover the lake's secrets.
She could dissolve her whiteness in its impartial surprise.
Her hair spread itself in a film of baroque longing.
This will be the guide to his confused eye, she thought.

Beneath the feet of a mother, the forest road waited.
A storm of dust veiled her from the suggestions all around.
The crevices of its forks could not consolidate her indecision.
She insisted, she insisted: only this dress, only this love!

The quarry widened to accept words of prayer.
Psalms gathered pink and urgent in the cracks in its marble walls.
Veins of silver indicated the appeal of ongoing pilgrimage.
How will we embrace the cool fires that engulf us, they wondered.

In the neighboring region, apples stood lined against white gates.
The means to a given beyond had long been established.
In the border region, a swaying motion somehow structured the terror.
But in the heart, the very eye, only a stillness.

א מאפע פֿון גערודער

אינעם אַרומיקן ראַיאָן האָבן זיך די בלעטער פֿון אַ וועלט צעוויקלט.
צווישן די מײַלער פֿון ביימער האָט מען אַלצדינג מסדר געווען.
דער שטעטל־זקנה האָט מען צוגעבראַכט עסן אָן קיין שום צרות.
קום, בחור, צו דער ליכט אין מײַנע פֿינגער, האָט זי געזאָגט.

אַ מיידל האָט פֿריַ אַנטדעקט די סודות פֿון דער אָזערע.
זי האָט געקענט צעלאָזן איר וויסקייט אין איר אומפֿאַרטייישן חידוש.
די האָר האָבן זיך צעשפּרייט אין אַ פֿילם פֿון באַראָקן בענקעניש.
דאָס וועט דינען זײַן צעמישטן אויג ווי אַ וועגווײַזער, האָט זי געטראַכט.

אונטער די פֿיס פֿון אַ מאַמען האָט דער וואַלדוועג געוואַרט.
אַ שטורעם פֿון שטויב האָט זי פֿאַרשלייערט פֿון די פֿירלייגן דאָ און דאָרט.
די שפּאַרעס פֿון זײַנע שיידוועגן האָבן נישט געקענט פֿאַרפֿעסטיקן איר אומבאַשלאָסנקייט.
זי האָט זיך אײַנגעשפּאַרט, זי האָט זיך אײַנגעשפּאַרט: נאָר דאָס קלייד, נאָר די ליבע!

די שטײַנערײַ האָט זיך פֿאַרברייטערט כּדי מקבל צו זײַן געבעטווערטער.
פּסוקי־תּהילים האָבן זיך געזאַמלט ראָז און אײַליק אין די שפּאַרונעס פֿון זײַנע מאַרמאָרנע ווענט.
אָדערן פֿון זילבער האָבן אָנגעוויזן אויף דעם צוצי פֿון כּסדרדיקער נסיעה.
ווי וועלן מיר אַרומנעמען די קילע פֿיַערן וואָס כאַפּן אונדז אַרום, האָבן זיי זיך געפֿרעגט.

אינעם שכניש ראַיאָן זײַנען עפּל געשטאַנען אַנטקעגן ווײַסע טויערן.
די מכשירים צו אַ געוויסן דערנאָך האָט מען לאַנג שוין געשאַפֿן.
אינעם גרענעץ־ראַיאָן האָט אַ שאָקל ווי ניט איז געמאַכט סדר פֿונעם טעראָר.
אָבער אין האַרצן, אין סאַמע אויג, נאָר אַ שטילקייט.

12

Stories Of Ida

For Hinde Ena Burstin

The Uriel Weinreich Program in Yiddish Language, Literature, and Culture, YIVO Institute for Jewish Research and Columbia University, 199-

The youth with the impossibly round glasses,
my absurdly spherical specs,
an aesthete on extended leave from rabbinical seminary,
curls matted in the detritus of long-
unconjugated irregular verbs,
murmurs on the return of ideology,
the vigor of the fast-approaching language wars.
His commentary sparks no immediate response,
only a passing of beans and rice from the off-off-campus co-op.
There's no need, it seems, no desire to fracture the taut serenity.
In strange agreement, Ida chooses to reflect not on the
trajectory between utopic imperative and cultural regeneration,
but on the Warsaw salon,
the threads between the patriarch
and the language poets' fragile courage.
It is in the crawlspaces between the bundles of photocopies
that she seeks to make room for our hopes.
Alerted by the romanticism of the afternoon's progression,
Reyzl interjects a note of muted stridency,
an insistence upon aims more utilitarian.
Entrance to tradition, sure, she allows,
but also simply a means,
one of many, like critical theory, that's all.
She used to see herself as a voice apart,
now she just wants to return to the text,
the limited certainty of the written.
Really, she's seen all of this positional reification before;
She's really just bored with her boredom.
Really.

Reaching for the grapes, Reyzl's linen sleeves trace
the re-emergent quiet and the trampled summer lawns beneath.
And in that moment,
shimmering unsteadily beyond the necessity of program brochure
and the inevitability of tableau,
the world is perfect.

Notes After Class: Red Autumn, 1987

For Stella Benakis and for Mike Marsico

If three early twenty-somethings,
grand/children of/ immigrants all,
huddled over a café table
could find a way to redeem the world,
we could have.
Surely ... well, maybe ...
But even then our goals were more attainable.
We only wanted to mine the varicose flashes of history,
hieroglyphs of an almost forgotten civilization.
How could words, imagined in isolation, we wondered,
expand into shared movement,
navigate the thwack of the police club on flesh
and the screams of horses galloping into crowds,
shape the persistence needed to render justice palpable?
How could we refashion ourselves in the gauze of banners past?

Forgive me then if the details are faded,
blurry upon excavation more than a generation later.

No surprise then that it is the intoxication of our expeditions
that has most remained
and the hunger that drove them forward.
Our conversations could not be contained
by the parameters of our course.
We skipped over the chasm in time and space to exhume
Eugene V., Mother J., Fannie Lou, Bayard,
and to imagine the unnamed and unremembered.
Then, decisions were fashioned from impossible choices.
Ideology was born of urgency, commitment, arrogance even,
but never of hairsplitting.
The poets, too, we observed, could not resist the molding of slogan,
the spare language of uprising, the austerity of platform.
For ourselves, we insisted, not on a pantheon,
but rather on extended families of the spirit, if not of blood.

Friends, comrades, we told each other,
this could be the Athens or Budapest or Turin
only barely imagined by our grandparents
or CCNY in the thirties.

But instead it was Philadelphia at little more than a decade from century's end.

And then too the portraiture of things—
for what an unlikely ensemble we were!
Stella, resplendent in long flowing black robes.
Mike, hair center-parted with round glasses gold-rimmed,
direct from the archives and yet utterly today.
I, with my yarmulke
and my earnestness, shiny and unvarnished:
tsedek tsedek tirdof[1] visualized for placards soon to be brandished.
Aware of the limitations of studiousness,
we could not help but note the boundaries of the frame around us, even then—
the going-through-photo-albums-in-the-attic-of it all.
Still, presentation was a signpost to interpretation. Wasn't it?

In those exchanges, murmured before departure
to the night shift in Ronald Reagan's America,
the impact of those sites—
Matewan, Ludlow, Haymarket, Patterson—
seared into us, chopping a swathe
towards something gorgeous and terrifying
and only dimly understood.
Uneasily, we realized that there could be no return
and girded ourselves to meet the oncoming scorn.
We could not re-bury these traces, our lost Atlantis.

---

1 *Tsedek tsedek tirdof (Deuteronomy 16:20): Justice justice ye shall pursue*

Skirts billowing, head lowered, leaflets fluttering into dusk,
Emma Goldman[2] walked with us in wordlessness to the El train.
The tingle of her touch, the catch of her sobs
hover around the scrim and scrawl of our engagements
long after her bent figure disappeared from view of the train
and the professor's posting of our final grade.

---

2 *Emma Goldman (1869-1940), anarchist, advocate for numerous causes, including women's rights*

Remembering Rosa Luxemburg In the "New" Times Square

Rosa[3], the porno theaters have vanished,
but the dreams remain.
They've only migrated from the realm of shadow
to the blare of billboards

The flashing lights reveal your face, exhausted after a rally,
        after yet another essay completed
            but
Rosa, I've lost the words to this poem.
I've lost my way to you.
Frantically, I've searched my old computer,
even the floppy disks. To no avail.
All I have are these lines scribbled down about

the scope of your vision,
your finely wrought theories,
now so buffeted by vogue winds
and the claims of identity politics and multiculturalism
        the singularity of your stances—
the courage of your opposition to the "Great War"
—the slaughter of workers everywhere—
even when others caved to the pressures of nationalism,
even when it landed you in prison,
your insistence on freedom and international solidarity and
democracy
even in revolution's heady throes,
your critique of Lenin's use of terror,
even as you knew what was to come,
those many years, sometimes with Leo[4], sometimes without him,
how the absence of his embrace could never deflect you for long,
truly a life in love and in struggle,
in loving struggle, in struggling love,
all of this, Rosa, has made its way into the memory halls of justice,

---

3 *Rosa Luxemburg (1871-1919), leader in European social democracy*
4 *Leo Jogiches (1867-1919), Luxemburg's comrade and lover*

into the meetings of the groups that trickle into basements
seeking somehow to end the carnage campaigns of today

and yes even if that very sweep erased the particular,
even if the interconnections of nation, minority, and self
never found footing in your analysis—
you, the immigrant from Poland,
the woman with a doctorate and a limp,
the Jew relentlessly attacked in anti-Jewish terms—
even if that. Still,

Rosa, you resist my rose-colored glasses.
Your ideas are too immense;
the events of your life are too neon—
from your revolutionary schoolgirlhood in Warsaw
to your corpse dumped in the Berlin canal after torture—
to be squeezed into a single soliloqu/ode,
even one this unkempt, this ungainly

So I summon you here,
              here,
beneath the claims for revolutionary bikini briefs
the announcements of new gadgets already outmoded,
the fabrication of craving for all things superfluous
the beams of searchlight oblivious to the sweatshops
and the sex slaves invisible to the dragons of clemency
and the homeless men shouting for retribution
and shelter and fifty cents
near the lone, if never lonely, military recruiting station
by the ruins of the glory holes and the ghosts of go-go boys perished,
I fondle the shards of my credit card, and I pause, gasping, to ask:

Rosa, Rosa, how did it come to this?

Fairground Evensong

I remember you the day we met,
how your eyes sang in the dusk,
how you bent to kiss the cotton candy with your daughter.
I distinguished the individual peals of your laughter in the carousel
        symphony,
followed your hair tickling the hallucinations of the plastic steed.

I remember you the day of the march across the bridge,
how you walked, the sureness of your grip on the placard,
how you smiled, joked, but only looked to the rally ahead, to
        resolution.
I found the crystalline thread of your chant amidst the others,
and I gripped it, rejecting the idea of release.

I remember you the day of my niece's birthday party,
how you knew exactly what to bring, how to present it to maximum
        enchantment,
how to pry wide the lips of the children and the parents.
I savored your hand, its shade canopy,
but I was able to let go, to rejoice in you across the cactus-filled
        living room.

I remember you the night I was led away,
how you captured the narrowed rhetoric of the day,
how you rebuffed the array of choices offered by the little man.
Instead, you invited me to lick biscotti crumbs from your neck.
Your breath snagged, warned me of footsteps in the corridor.

I remember you from this cage, these nights and days infinite,
how you would not sob or scream,
how you would not slump or turn away.
I clutch your gaze, the ferocity of your belief as long as I can, always.
I cradle you now against the man shivering below and the dogs
        frothing overhead.

The Last Music Lesson

Even with tanks on the city's threshold
and panic clotting the shops,
she still had to go.
Her mother's blandishments on the enduring power of art and so on
ringing in her ear,
she trudged up the stairs,
that refugee flight winding upwards into suffocation.
His wince in place, the tutor held the door open and
gestured ironically to the instrument of torment.
She began to clatter away, horrified by the sound as ungainly
as her body, trying desperately to muffle them both.
What connection could any of this have to the words
"allegro" and "andante" and "arpeggio" that her mother clutched
against book burnings and broken glass?
The tutor glanced out the window
as a different sort of banging continued its bleak momentum.
He would have to move again, he realized absently.
From the corner of her eye, she glimpsed a newly placed photo
of a young woman attired so:

Tuxedo, top hat above cropped hair, gloves, cane, carnation, dazzle

She ceased her racket, jolted by a realization of her own
and an unfamiliar sense of possibility.
Following her gaze, the tutor murmured,
"My daughter" and smiled.
She saw him for the first time without his armor
and blurted her gratitude.
Knowing she would never see him again,
she fled past his now stooped frame
down the stairs into the empty streets.
And with music in her heart at last,
she welcomed the apocalypse and her path through its fires.

Cat Lady's Request

Forget it all, every last wisp.
It can't be recalled, anyway.
The quest for antecedent,
for the contours of primordial meat dumpling,
for the steps marched en route to annihilation,
however noble, is doomed, in the end.
Don't imagine otherwise. Don't be lulled
by branches waltzing along on gray silk,
by the ache of your blurry yearning,
into conclusions of grandeur or imagined connection.

Pulp the maps and the guidebooks;
burn the photo albums.
Circumvent the archives,
municipal and otherwise.
Why face the natives pissing at the tour bus?
Don't go to the tombstones,
tottering in drunken gloom.
You won't find anything.
I come from the garden of nothing and nowhere,
and to there I shall return.
You too, you know.

Still, if anything should happen to me in the by and by,
she paused,
her many chins aquiver at last,
peering through the lace of bramble and tangle,
take care of my children.
This one is X,
and this here is the angel Y,
my twin integers against the apocalypse.
That's all I ask. And thank you for visiting.
Come see us again soon.

Awards Night Apparition

Below the palms trembling against the confectionary buildings
the whispering climbing into exclamation
the glamourati assembled to celebrate themselves
the curiosity over shade and flair and form
who was wearing what by whom
after all the stakes couldn't be more elusive
so that the carpet seemed bloody rather than red
and the poses not struck but entered embodied
so effortless unstudied all this had to seem
for there was little time so impatient were the cameras' clicks
when she appeared in her tatters mousy no dun-colored
barn-scented hunched over
but also swelling outward looking upward
her hair tangled her eyes bulging and her nostrils shivering
and no one could ascertain her objectives
was she in costume if not then was she protesting and if so
should they mention her cause in their acceptance speeches
several gladly volunteered to do so once they learned more of course
only her cane shook wildly so they had to duck
with care paid however gingerly to chignon and bauble
and her speech was unintelligible garbled
what language was this if any
and they began to move outward until security thank goodness
arrived and surrounded to whisk her away
only it was not so easy there was tenacity in her frame
and enduring power an eerie pattern to her movement and words
almost beginning to be recognizable
stirring something familiar dimly remembered
only finally she really was off the carpet now somehow soiled
and the screens beaming into the infinite
and everyone shook their heads uneasily
hoping this wasn't some kind of
foreshadowing or terrorism or a warning of retribution
from the unamused gods of the netherworld

Spinster's Lament

The painting of the rabbi purchased from the homeless man
        (on 6th Avenue for $10) his
prayer shawl framing eyes frowning upon my barrenness

The pea green vase purchased on the streets of Columbus Circle
        (with its "Made in Italy" stamp on the bottom) thinking
probably it wasn't but savoring still its roundness, its squat insistence

The stained china cup, with its pattern of irises
        (at once delicate and modernist) from
which I sipped and struggled to master the edicts of my fathers

That copy of Kenneth Clark's *The Nude* that I spotted as the 4 o'clock
        light poured in (through the trees of Tompkins Square)
shadowing your shoulders arched over turrets of military history tomes

The Jenny Lind bed rescued from that barn in the Finger Lakes
        (nearly asphyxiated by rat droppings and dust) where
you loved me with such focus that one November night

The Psalms I clutched as I slithered into the Ukrainian Church
        (from the downpour after our last pierogi lunch) and
murmured feverishly to foreign, equally indifferent gods

The quilt, never littered with cat hair, wrapped around my sensible
        frame (those decades of Decembers) even
as I prepared for the arrival of the chariot drawn by bejeweled stallions

Who will cherish the provenance of these objects?

Who will say Kaddish for me when I'm gone?

What Agnès Whispered

(severely or so it seemed initally) in the corridor
under the Tina Modotti[5] poster *Tinisima!*
after the guests had departed the dinner party
which I thought had gone smashingly
everything so scrumptious and almost everyone so repartee-ful
and assured her thus much to her delight
so that she conceded a smile
she couldn't begrudge me that
and her blush from July itself
but more from the triumph of it all mounted one shade roser
so adorable is she to me I did truly want to kiss her
and she said thanks thanks so much for coming for helping
for navigating the cliques for melting some of the frost
but I noticed something in your eye she continued
the consternation when you saw Klára again with Anna
don't try to hide or deny it you can't I saw it
don't think you know it all how to say don't *assume* that
because Klára can't sail or even plod through the topics of the day
or even that she always seems so glazed over
appears eager to leave seems removed behind a sheer of indifference
revives only when the talk turns to literary gossip
don't assume you know what happens when their door closes
when their lights are dimmed when she and Anna return to ease
without the need for chatter bright and glossy and pointed
don't assume you no *we* can ever understand
the shape of that transition
the specificity of her limbs entwined with Anna's
the contours of their together lips
their hair braided fleetingly in restlessness
her hands locked over Anna's mouth over Anna's wrists
don't think we have lost Anna
or that she is no longer ours a part of us
don't mourn the disappearance of the old Anna
our hikes in the mountains our walks through galleries
our laughing on the last ride of the night Ferris wheel

---

5 *Tina Modotti (1896-1942), photographer, model, actress, revolutionary*

our demonstrations in the plaza outside the embassy
our arrest that night together in the cell with its unmentionables
however absorbed however now distilled disheveled distracted
don't even think there is an Anna of yore
only know this is still our Anna this is the only Anna
we must stay with her

Come Hear the Fat Lady Sing

This poem encounters the fat lady long after her transformation.
You can hear bubbles of accordion music
through the din of the crumpling tent. Even in the murky light,
it's clear that she has just finished a performance.
Reluctantly, the fat lady swats away the pancake make-up.
She moans happily, as she recalls the screeches of delight
when she wiggled her colossal fanny.
She can still feel the hard pokes of the children,
probing her many folds as she beckoned them closer.
She chastised the parents for pulling their young ones away,
chuckling, *it's just a bit of fun really,*
winking, *I ain't gonna smother them, you know.*
Hmmm, she sighs, kissing the mirror, *that was a good show.*

As the fat lady removes her robes, those vast, undulating sheets,
you might step a bit closer, just to get a closer look.
Don't be afraid. No, don't look there!
If you look deeply, searchingly into her eyes,
you'll see a very different fat lady.
You'll see her, hunched over, eyes downcast.
She's wearing billowing elephant-colored drapes down Main Street,
where she goes only when her mother forces her to fetch the groceries.
The hooligans shout names and obscenities. No surprise there.
The girls turn away, terrified of contagion.
The women cluck in pity; the men smile and wink and stare.
Everyone has something to say or do; she is a spectacle,
No, a public commodity. Only no one's bidding. Why should they?

It is important for you to glimpse that time.
But don't let's focus on it.
Let's return instead to the dank dressing room where we began.
And no, I won't tell you how she got from there to here,
although I know you probably want to know.
The fat lady has just put on her bloomers.
She's found a green velvet cape in the mountain of costumes.
It'll be perfect tonight over her black dress, she thinks.

She hears whispering about "development" and "gentrification."
In response, the fat lady farts with gusto. She will not be worried.
If she loses this fat lady position, there will always be others.
She surveys the bank of bouquets choking her table,
a few still surprisingly spry in the heat.

She removes a sunflower for the dwarf, who waits outside her door.
They detect dissonant melodies and fiery stars bobbing across the
        plains.
Clutching him against her bosom,
the fat lady lumbers to join the procession just underway.

The Blind Man In the Arms Of the Prostitute

Never had he been touched so.
In fact, it had been decades since he'd been touched at all.
Usually it was he who touched others—
grasping the back of shoulders, exploring a face,
shaping a line and curve with his feathery touch.
He had found his way to her door from memory
etched in a time when purpose had been evident,
when he could do certain things,
because this is the way open to men.
Perhaps because of the respect accorded his former self—
the flaneur, the man-about-town—
or the breadth accorded his current self—
the shuttered eyes, the cautious step—
discretion remained an option for him.
No gaze followed him, he knew this.

Never had she been touched so.
She loathed the platitudes assembled to categorize
the histories of those in her work—
the prison of the profile.
But she could not derail the trajectory,
the momentum of its apparent inevitability:
the invasions of the brothers by narrow daylight,
the fumbling of the father at midnight,
the men on the side of the road,
until finally here, still so young,
but with a roof over her head, at least.
It's ok for now, she told herself,
until she found something else.
And she would find something else, she knew that.

When he entered her room, she did not even look up.
Only his paralysis by the door elicited her call from the pillows
and then her rising to guide him to her bed.
His fingers found light in the embers of her skin;
her pores opened to his caress.

Her fingers traveled over his body, long underused but still so supple;
his limbs melded with her body,
long used but suddenly aglow from gentleness.
The weight of his coerced passivity and her coerced activity,
the anguish of their losses were momentarily lifted.
Enfolded in her embrace, grunts audible through the shivering walls,
he whispered, "Thank you for this seeing."
She replied into his neck, something fervent, unintelligible.
But her face, luminous in the window, visible somehow to him
as he departed down the alley, explained it all.

Border Crossing: Corridor, 7:35 p.m.

hours after work's close
i stumble from light's drone
from navigating processing information jigsaw
the disappointment of volumes yet to be added
and author name headings still unreconciled

past the cleaning lady in the hall
furrowed over the cart of industrial hygiene
bleach mops cleaners suds powders
soaps toilet paper paper towel
all things familiar yet rendered other on this epic scale

her ankles thickened from long standing
her hands gloveless swollen from scrubbing
her wrists free of ornament
her body wrapped in sack and apron
her hair caged in netting

and i remember college jobs of housecleaning
how i relished the solitude the absence of overseer
the peering into the nooks of strangers' secrets
the money for books once even an early Jean Rhys[6] first edition
the deliverance however fleeting from my father's mounting
          consternation

and think how different this is for her
these hours days years stretching into endless
of scouring and wiping and rinsing
the waste of these bookish others
of mine this life in not quite shadow

but still the satisfaction or perhaps something like it
the dignity resisting heroic
in task completed

---

6 *Jean Rhys (1890-1979), author of such novels as* After Leaving Mr.
Mackenzie *and* Wide Sargasso Sea

in the sparkle of these post-happy hour toilets
and the clean of this federal marble

and i wonder about origins
cracked earth crowded rooms
the likelihood of instruction
and the terror of leaving love and language
being nearly buried alive in car trunk

and hope for the kiss of a child
the embrace of a man or woman at dance
cavorting of tiger lily in kitchen window
chorus of cricket on the green
and the cheer of souls clapping in communion

as I sound my evening adieu
and am gladdened by her looking up at me
by her smile suddenly so radiant by her clarity
and think I have been all wrong all wrong maybe
and step on yet unwashed tiles into elevator's arms

Counter-History

Rahel Bluwstein (1890-1931), Hebrew Poet

If Rahel had lived longer,
would she have reconsidered a sojourn in Italy,
to reflect on questions of aesthetics and living among the nations,
would she have returned to work in the fields,
enlarged by the surge of green, by the earth's cadences,
would she have continued to work with children,
sustained by sheperding the advance to understanding?

If Rahel had lived longer,
If her days had not ended, after wandering, in a tubercular room,
would she have known the lingering embrace of the beloved,
would she have been replenished by young laughter,
would she have broadened her lens from the self to the world,
would her tones have increased in delicacy in the gleam of years,
Could she have discovered joy in the passing away of sun?

If Rahel had lived longer,
would her lyric still have traveled into and onto countless tongues,
would they still have been transformed by unforeseen music,
reborn under the tenderness of strange hand,
would pilgrims still flock to her stone by the sea,
reverently removing the book from the little box,
Would her words have engraved their way into eternity?

To the Poet, No Longer Young, Introverted By Nature

If literature, despite Oprah, thrives at the margins,
yours is surely the most marginal of the literary arts.
You provide no PowerPoint, no slide show.
You resist props and elucidation.
You claim no expertise, no decades in archives,
no power to foam or foment on talk radio or cable television.

And even among your peers,
you will never work a room, you will never master
the between-poem patter, the strategically placed joke.
Awkward at gatherings where such skills are honed,
never having undergone the camps and factories,
yours will be a path of stone and struggle.

But the example of Emily Dickinson is no option, either.
The life of seclusion, reified in the rarefied home
and forever in legend, cannot be yours.
You know this, even if after these many years,
your audiences grow no larger,
and the solitary chamber seems increasingly seductive.

Speak your words with precision, without adornment.
As they foray into the room, let the quiet be their guide.
The bob of the head, the intake of breath
will sustain their navigation.
Cherish the frail woman sitting in the back, eyes wide until the end,
and afterwards, the dry hands clasped around your damp ones,

as you descend the stairs toward the street lamp-lit bus ride home.

Smitten

For Sylvia Poggioli, NPR Reporter

No byline is required.
Your voice,
flinty, lean,
can never be mistaken,
commands attention.
Under your spell everything slows to the opposite of languor.

The sounds of you evoke
smoke-filled rooms, where destinies are determined,
heels clicking on marble-tiled corridors,
gazing at the stars on a trans-Atlantic deck while big band glistens
          below,
fountain angels offering water dappled in late afternoon sun,
burgundy sipped while glancing occasionally, casually at a wristwatch,
fat cats ducking back into offices,
women insisting their way in the world,
like Beverly Gray in the books my sister and I shared years ago.

Whenever I chance to marvel at
the architecture of your dispatches,
so direct, yet so intricate,
constructed with such care,
I imagine all that is possible in an indifferent universe,
that human frailty can be fathomed,
however momentarily.
I can finger the drama of narrative being shaped;
I can enter the whirl, seemingly in mid-spin.

And so, with anchored heart,
hunched over toiletry,
toothbrush in hand, espresso rising nearby,
I venerate your determination, and again, your voice,
and the medium also, still sprightly, that propels you forth.
And Sylvia, I vow to send a donation in the next pledge drive.

Fag Hag and Fag, Approaching Daybreak

her mouth slack
arms paused in mid-flail
curls sprawled on the embroidery-bordered pillow
without perspiration in this bedroom without relief of air movement
breath rising evenly having returned somewhat early
from Balkan dancing or perhaps salsa
pirouetting between shifting nations of desire
he sits in quiet jarred from fragile somnia
on the chair by her mirror below the black and white photos
and the shrine of East European guidebooks and maps
the old country tapestries invigorated in the receding nocturne
and gazes upon her oh-how-well-he-knows outline
but then bends to trace his fingers on her skin
electrified by its smoothness softness
uninterrupted by thoughts of experience
their thrift shopping expeditions
their world music concertizing art films the travel the phone calls
the talk always the talk hours passing passed the dance halls
the Friday night pierogi dinners surrounded by hipsters and Slavs
this love that can't be depicted by lists of activities
or measured by the quivering of landmarks but only by
pleasure deepening joy expanding loyalty unflagging
over the years the good times
and the hard times as they say yes those too
tricky to put decades into words these few
but also the men hers the excitement determination
trying to be open but still with etiquette observed upheld
the feminist thrilled by chivalry
oh how he would love to be a fly on the wall
(there's just no other way to say it) on those dates
or an undercover agent in black a few tables away
his head lowered
braving some noxious brew to hear
willing her their conversation well she and this new man
attraction to be mutual urgent rising into transcendence enduring

never mind whether she can bring him home to Father
may this man be the one for her
and yes hoping too there will still be a place for him
not a threesome but the proverbial chair at the table
or somewhere in the house in any case
he can't not think about that how could he not
only instead he's here stroking a lock from her face
as she murmurs tosses to the other side
as he returns to her bed neither maidenly nor nuptial
grateful for this sanctuary between dreams and his resting angel

On Rejection: A Valentine

What is this animal determination,
the ox at the plow stabbing parched earth?
Why slog through the desert towards some mirage of clarity,
gasping for words to embody the inchoate,
ones perhaps better left in the smog of pre-birth?

When the gulls skimming the river's façade beckon to flight,
and flamenco heels rain click-clack on mahogany expanse,
when,
instead of dust clouds,
I might whisper through magnolias to muslin ones overhead?

What is this resolve to send forth?
Famished for approval stingily parsed,
scanning the mail late to arrive, if ever it does.
Learning to foresee the envelopes' contents by their weight—
the morsels whose import I've trained years to minimize.

When the potter's hands coax the clay into gleam,
and the scent of chocolate mousse pie wafts from Esperanza's oven,
when,
instead of fragments of indifference,
a parchment scroll hand-painted with cherry blossom pastoral
          unfolds?

Reader, I know only this:

The lilt of choreographed words pierces the density of July insomnia.
When nocturnal forays conclude in blank smile,
leaving me to dodge the menace simmering from boozy street quarrel,
these words greet me, accompany me to the vacant bed,
train my heart to rearrange its girdle.

So I assemble all the rejection missives, weave them into a coverlet—
to the east, those from the glossy weekly;
to the west, those from the aloof monthly—
a source of respite from dirt and plow, signifiers all of song
resounding somehow, some way, someday into attentive night.

Hebrew Lullaby

Under the weight of July's first swelter,
I greeted the rosary beads of verbs.

Here, as I lay inert—a stifled vulgarity—
came words of relief, a reservoir of linguistic lemonade.

Against the tear of flesh, the wail of witness,
these other sounds somehow bore me aloft: *shamati, shamata*[7] ...

If I could have pooled white sands, caressed the stones of Rachel,
would my skin have then gained insight?: *nagati, nagata*[8] ...

When the palm fronds of my beard became encrusted with
       pomegranate juice,
even as I got caught in puddles of milk and honey: *akhalti, akhalta*[9] ...

There, our bodies would surely assume armors of gleam,
negotiate a changed economy of utopic forms: *nashamti, nashamta*[10] ...

How then to forge a clearing in the forest of lost signs and rebuffed
       longing?
Of what use the indifference of summer tenement walls?

Still, a reluctant solace emerges. Above the frame of my conjugation
       bed,
the bedrock of my ancient insomnia: *ani nah, ani nah.* I rest! I rest!

---

7 *shamati, shamata:* I heard, you heard
8 *nagati, nagata:* I touched, you touched
9 *akhalti, akhalta:* I ate, you ate
10 *nashamti, nashamta:* I breathed, you breathed

העברעיִש וויגליד

אונטער דער וואָג פֿון יולים ערשטער חמימה,
האָב איך באגרייסט די פֿאטשערקעס פֿון ווערבן.

דאָ בשעת כ'לייג זיך אינערט — אַ דערשטיקטע וווּלגאַרקייט —
זײַנען געקומען ווערטער פֿון הילף, אַ רעזערוואַר פֿון שפּראַכיקן לימענאַד.

אַנטקעגן דעם ריס פֿון הויט, דער יללה פֿון עדות זאָגן,
האָבן אָט די אַנדערע קלאַנגען מיך ניט ווי ניט אויפֿגעהויבן: שמעתי, שמעת ...

אויב כ'וואָלט דעמאָלט געקענט צונויפֿנעמען ווייסע זאַמדן, גלעטן רחלס שטיינער,
וואָלט דאָס מײַן הויט פֿאַרשטאַנען? נגעתי, נגעת ...

ווען די לולבֿים פֿון מײַן באָרד זײַנען קלעפֿיק געווען מיט מילגרוימזאַפֿט,
אַפֿילו ווען איך בין געבליבן שטעקן אין קאַלוושעס פֿון מילך און האָניק: אכלתי, אכלת ...

דאָרטן וואָלטן אונדזערע גופֿים זיכער אָנגעטאָן פֿאַנצערס פֿון גלאַנץ,
פֿאַרהאַנדלט אַ נײַע עקאָנאָמיע אוטאָפֿישע פֿאַרמען: נשמתי, נשמת ...

ווי קען מען שאַפֿן אַ פֿאַליאַנע אין אַ וואַלד פֿון פֿאַרלוירענע סימנים און אָפֿגעשטויסן בענקעניש?
צו וואָס דער גלײַכגילט פֿון זומערדיקע טענעמענט-הײַזערוווענט?

פֿאָרט קומט אַרויס אומגערן אַ טרייסט. אַריבער דער ראַם פֿון מײַן קאָניוגאַציע בעט,
דעם מוטערשטײַן פֿון מײַן אַנטיקן אומשלאָף. אני נח. אני נח. כ'רו! כ'רו!

41

II

Men

Instead Of a Manifesto

He opened the door with trepidation.
In such matters the patriarch had not been economical,
although back then it was called "awe."
The door made no noise; he entered quietly.
(He had, of course, already mastered the art of stealth.)

But there was no need to worry.
No horn blew; no lightning descended.
No one even noticed his entry.
In the room stood a few pieces of furniture: a bed, a table, a chair.
(For these things he traveled so far?)

Before removing his shoes, he looked outside,
just to observe his new surroundings.
But he saw nothing of note:
a canopy of fog, and behind, a network of starry fragments.
(No matter—as long as he could rest.)

All the debates—great vs. minor, death vs. renaissance—
which had once burned so fiercely, fell away.
What impact could they have against these dense walls?
The burden of authenticity fled to a neighboring courtyard.
He removed his shoes.

But old walls, however dense, cannot repel everything.
Sometimes he saw the words of a poster,
sometimes the crumbs of a picnic.
Once he thought he heard a man's laugh.
He immediately brushed it off.

The truth is that footsteps did sometimes pass by his room.
And several did enter, as stealthily as he himself.
But except for an occasional nocturnal outing he never left.
All that he required he had by his side: a few verses,
a necklace of whispers, and the north winter light of language.

אנשטאָט אַ מאַניפֿעסט

ער האָט געעפֿנט די טיר מיט מורא.
אין אַזעלכע ענינים האָט דער טאַטע נישט געזשאַלעוועט
כאַטש דעמאָלט האָט מען דאָס אָנגערופֿן „יראה.".
קיין רעש האָט די טיר נישט געמאַכט; גנבֿיש איז ער אַריין.
(די קונסט פֿון גנבֿישקייט האָט ער שוין, פֿאַרשטייט זיך, באַהערשט.)

אָבער ער האָט זיך נישט געדאַרפֿט זאָרגן.
קיין שופֿר האָט מען נישט געבלאָזן;
קיינער האָט אַפֿילו נישט באַמערקט זיַן אַריַינקום.
אינעם צימער זיַנען געשטאַנען עטלעכע שטיקער מעבל: אַ בעט, אַ טיש, אַ בענקל.
(צוליב אָט די זאַכן איז ער אַזוי ווײַט געפֿאָרן?)

פֿאַרן אויסטאָן די שיך האָט ער אַ קוק געטאָן אין דרויסן
פשוט צו זען וואָס סע טוט זיך אין דער ניַער סבֿיבֿה.
אָבער ער האָט גאָרנישט נישט געזען:
אַ חופֿה פֿון נעפּל, אַ נעץ פֿון שטערנישע פֿראַגמענטן.
(נישט וויכטיק – אַבי מע רוט זיך אָפּ.)

אַלע וויכוחים – עיקר כנגד טפֿל, טויט כנגד ווידערווווקס –
וואָס האָבן אַ מאָל געפֿלאַקערט אַזוי שטאַרק זיַנען אווועקגעפֿאַלן.
וואָס פֿאַר אַ טרעף האָבן זיי געקענט מאַכן אויף די דיקע שטיינערנע ווענט?
דער עול פֿון אויטענטישקייט איז אַנטלאָפֿן אין אַ שכניש הויף.
ער האָט זיך אויסגעטאָן די שיך.

אָבער אַלטע ווענט, כאַטש געדיכט, קענען נישט אַלץ אָפּטריַיבן.
אַ מאָל האָט ער געזען ווערטער אויף אַ פּלאַקאַט,
אַ מאָל די ברעקלער פֿון אַ פּיקניק.
אײַן מאָל האָט זיך אים געדאַכט אַז ער הערט דאָס געלעכטער פֿון אַ מאַן.
ער האָט דאָס תּיכּף אווועקגעמאַכט.

דעם אמת געזאָגט, זיַנען טריט יאָ פֿאַרבַיַי זיַן צימער.
און עטלעכע זיַנען יאָ אַריַין, גנבֿיש ווי ער אַליין.
אָבער אַחוץ אַ זעלטענעם נאָכטיקן אַרויספֿאַר איז ער בכלל נישט אַרויס.
וואָס ער האָט נאָר געדאַרפֿט איז ביַי אים געווען צו דער האַנט: אַ פֿאָר פּסוקים,
אַ האַלדזבאַנד פֿון שושקענען, און די צפֿון־ווינטערל־ליכט פֿון לשון.

Smoke From Mirrors/Ruins Under the Roller Coaster

Was it the unfamiliar streets,
engulfed by whisper, a labyrinth of uncertainty.

Once I might have traveled this terrain:
the shifting curtains, hair brushed from eyes, fences rising brusquely.

But we had never needed the instruments of navigation;
we alone had been the cartographers of these fields.

Our hands had cut through the vines of resistance;
at the opposite end of the world, I heard your voice.

How then are these planets aligned?
Who ensures the edge of this line, the symmetry of these red rings?

Outside the elevated train, an entire cityscape bore witness. Even
without our visibility, the skyscrapers divined the intricacy of our
            need.

These pages were not torn; these words were not muffled.
Through the day's expansion, this had been no frail articulation.

Despite my entreaties, my insistence on the known city, I was
            whisked,
captive of your whim and whimsy, into an abruptly invoked carnival.

And it was there, in that frayed underworld, with its mirages and
            riddles,
that I lost sight of you, your undiminished locks, your thick neck, in
            the corridor of mirrors

and sat frozen instead on the carousel, unable to disentangle from
tinny music, unable to disembark from sticky plastic horse.

But surely that vanishing could never have been foreseen;
all steps could not have led to this absence of insight, this ashy
            oblivion.

Eventually the children returned to chant against the oncoming
     Coney Island dark,
and heeding the clarity of their call, I stumbled from the shimmering
     wreckage.

I had no choice. Refusing the veil of mangled cotton candy,
I glided into the sheath of my solitude, the thorn carpet of my
     without-you.

Ménagerie à Trois, Or, Having It Out With Man's Best Friend

When Caleb entered me,
my eyes met Elliot's.
For a moment those eyes reassured me,
apparent guarantors of an unforbidden pleasure.
I opened myself further and folded my limbs
around Caleb's glistening ones above,
porous to the changing rhythms of a newly plausible universe.
But suddenly Elliot's fur stood on end.
His growl transitioned into a cacophony of barks;
his body poised to pounce.
But I refused Elliot's fury and despair,
only welcoming Caleb further into me.
I clung to his back and ran through its fields of muscle;
I imagined the solo tango of my favorite mole in its very center.
There I lay, shielded by Caleb's strength
and the growing intensity of his grunts,
as my mind darted over last night's dishes, an online petition,
and the progress of the seemingly eternal subway track repair.
There was so much to keep track of!
And in this stasis of languid panic
I floated until Caleb's final giving way.
As he lay spent above me,
I noted Elliot's cunning new tactic—the whimper—
and observed Caleb's hand reach over to stroke him,
a movement ominously foreshadowing
the coming alignment of this triangle.

Walking With Sarina

All the schoolyard taunts initially came to mind:
He—beanpole, tower, tree trunk, ropy, Lincoln, skyscraper, pillar.
(But now with a twist—the ripple of sinew, the strain of bicep.)
And she far below—a speck, paramecium, toy, bobble-head, Weeble.
An odd couple, sure, but also wondrous to behold.

With Sarina, you see, Marvin made sense.
His long limbs formed a fortress around her barkless muzzle,
her tiny body—more places to hide, snuggle, get warm, even in
        summer.
A light bore through her rheumy eyes at his approach.
His every move, his very touch transformed her into ecstasy.

With Sarina, Marvin removed his mantle of self-deprecation,
the voices from long ago, the stares of today.
In the fog of her declining breath, he could loosen the fortress of
        his discipline.
Hovering around his ankles, her limp was if not healed, then
        irrelevant.
Her wiry gray curls became damask under his massive hands.

Throughout their strolls the neighbors eyed, not the tower and the
        toy,
but me, the one behind them. It was so obvious: none of this was
        about me.
Even when Marvin pooled Sarina's drool and I saw myself
hobbling to the toilet of an old age home—
a scrim on the eyelids banished to the cobwebs of foreshadow, even
        then I knew this.

So don't let this poem be about me, the ghostly lover outside the
        frame.
If you have to see me here at all, see me not as interloper,
but as chronicler of a gentle love. Listen to me as I walk with them,
whispering my incantation, my mantra of well-wishing:
Sarina, Serena, serene, serenity, Sarina, Serena, serenity, serene …

To the Soldier, Sitting Opposite On the Riverdale Bound Train

Where I had been riding on my journey, eager for inspiration
sought from the formal (and casual) gardens and the views of the river
whose more distant reaches had inspired so many others,
my favorite temple that required a worship of its own
but no rules of dress or dues,
where the only hymn was the rustle of green and violet into wind,
the excited cry of the child and the reprimand sure-to-follow,
this place, a sanctuary for my elusive tranquility,
as if this were the Lake District
and I a latter-day prophet of Arcadia,
all of this so close I could taste
the verdancy, the roll of that very word in my famished cosmos …

Until the soldier sat down across from me,
with his brilliant Adam's apple
and his thickness pressing everywhere against his uniform,
taking me to that instantaneous other hunger
so that I didn't know where to place my eye or my tongue or my legs
and so I turned away but saw him again, in the window, only this
        time,
with greater clarity, turned now
on the gun that was not next to him,
on the tanks that did not rumble outside,
on the failed precision of all the missiles,
on the nighttime raids in the eerie green light, that other green light,
on the parents huddled in grief at summer dusk
on the flaking front porch

And even though his countenance resisted my narratives
and his impassivity buffeted my parade of imagery,
the bramble of my musings
on the nature of nationalism, the peculiarities of opportunity,
the strange mixture of the immediate and the impervious that resulted
in his sitting here, in this uniform, on this train, across from me,
and even though the paths of Jewish history

do not necessarily converge at pacifism,
I wanted only to embrace him, to implore him:
disembark with me, instead,
Come, like others before you, to these gardens,
restore yourself in the generosity of this light,
remember, now, the power of our shared origins
and, always, this train ride as the arbiter of our transformed world.

Voyeur's Diary

How he loved the flashes of things:
the wink of construction worker ass crack above boxer shorts
the tightening of muscled neck as head turns to study ephemeral
        booty
the thicket of underarm hair while coffee is swigged from metal
        thermos
sweaty tufts peering below the hard hat

How he savored the hints of things:
the swell of the commuter's suit pants on the crowded subway
the taper of the back below fitted poplin shirt
the leather messenger bag creating valleys in shoulders evenly forged
legs planted wide against the train's lurch

Visual skills first learned in high school were honed in later years:
the mastery of the concealed glance, the sculpting of desire almost
        visible.
In another era his might have become the scribblings of
the solitary and plain young man,
longing poured into notebook below locks shading averted eyes.

But in this era of plague and disquiet, he had become yet another
bubble boy, notes in hand, glimpses collected in mind,
one of the legions seen bobbing at the edges of the boulevards
of the metropolis, sealed from the invasion of the virus into body
and the tongue of dreams tickling a passageway into innermost ear.

Bodies On Fire

Sometimes over gay lunch
a friend will tell
of someone he's seen in the shower
or the locker room
he'll say
hey listen politics of objectification aside
you should have seen his butt—
to die for
conversation drifts on
though I become quiet
at the words
the invoking of willed mortality
because

when I'm in those spaces
I glimpse—
through the vapor of
hushed accusation (cousins not called for)
and "the motion picture event of the year"—
balls dangling low
under floppy cocks
conspicuously cut
and expanses of sagging
and sinuous flesh
so vulnerable
when
they bend down
to pull on
their underpants

all nice and clean
and ready for
the gas chambers

Diner Doodles

1.

What if the cock,
like the belly,
expanded with age?

And if it did,
would it be as desirable?

2.

Does a man-hating dog
snarl at a male-to-female transsexual in transition?

And if it does,
at what point in the process does its aggression cease?

On the Threshold Of Utopia

Sojourns in the worlds of Kristen Bjorn

Here no one has trouble getting it up
or getting it in.
There's no frustration,
no wincing,
no screaming,
no weeping,
no turning away.

Bodies are shared, taken smoothly.
One out, the next in.
All is choreographed in geometric form
designed for display of maximum limberness—
gymnastic sex, bodybuilder sex, ballet sex,
always with equal degree of effortlessness.
Threesomes never become twosomes.

Men, some sculpted, some sleek, some bulging,
all differently breathtaking, glide through
plush locales—tropical jungles, ancient villages,
waterfalls, carefully appointed villas, ruins—
moaning in foreign, largely unsubtitled tongues,
except for the interludes that frame the bacchanalia.
Sometimes, even after all the orgies, guy gets guy.

In an economy of scarcity,
here glitters a fairy tale world of abundance,
devoid of restraint or retribution.
Here, our archetypes are reflected back at us,
scar, wart, and blemish miraculously excised.
Knowing we can never partake,
we see what is possible and can't look down, either.

Without ticket or means of entry,
we bathe in the flicker of glory and tedium.
We dangle in a purgatory of spectatorship,
eager for, yet forever postponing, the Eden of release.
Until finally we have to mop up
and stagger off to flimsy forgetting,
to the canopy of tender nocturne.

Rendezvous With the Angel

Vinnie D'Angelo, Hot House Exclusive

I dreamed I met Vinnie D'Angelo tonight.

I fell prostrate before his divinity,
eyes averted from the sure-to-be-stern gaze and
in advance of the command:

Assume the position, son.

This one is for the lipstick you "borrowed" from your sister.
This one is for the flowered sun frock you wore to Yiddish class.
This one is for all the hazelnut gelato devoured on Yom Kippur.
This one is for the Talmudic tractates you failed to master.
This one is for all of the tithes not taken.
This one is for the times you looked upon me, discharging yourself
        into dissipation.
This one is for all the other cocks, the battering against textual
        sanction.
This one is for the Sabbath labor, the savaging of sacred rest.
This one is for the disgrace you've brought to the house of Israel.
This one is for …

"Please, angel, have mercy," I implored,
as his whip scorched my flesh,
as the welts scattered,
as the blood oozed,
even as he continued,
and I lost track of my infractions,
even then I never stopped beseeching.

Only when he re-assembled me in his arms,
the sweat gushing from his harness,
and licked my head with his beard
and kissed my cheeks, only then did I realize

that my sorrow had been, if not lifted, then somehow moved,
that my devotion had at least been noted by the heavenly
interlocutor.

I dreamed I met Vinnie D'Angelo tonight.
Vincent of the Angels, the Angel Vincent, *l'angelo Vincente*.

Prayer For the Way/ward

as he crosses the threshold
sinking into the carpet
and absorbs the mod chairs
and the lamps shuttered and the canvases inscrutable
and the hulk of leather couch crouching
all so crisp and blank
no sign of danger …
yet

after only a brief conversation
driven by his starvation
to touch and smell and sweat and be exhilarated
to be released on furlough from the hovel of his loneliness
something about complementary interests
or compatibility
that element whose import grows
as its fruition becomes more elusive

as he looks up to behold the objective of his visit
decades in the dungeon gym gleaming whitely
all the ridges and curves and bulges
in all the right places just so
the wonder of him as promised a mere hour ago
even without pix sent
or telephone number given
so driven was he

as he falls to his knees
let there be no sharp or blunt instrument overhead
no sledgehammer chainsaw razor blade nothing
to reconfigure this encounter or him altogether
let there be no theft no diminishing
but only these unnamed bodies coming together
only this movement of limb into pleasure
only return to haven and soon soon home

Street Lamp Revelation

This is a poem for those who call and arrange the room
(and for those who answer the call, check the calendar)

For those who make sure the guest speaker can come and has a place
to stay after a trickle of messages tepid with indecision and
      postponement.

This is a poem for those who craft the flyer text, who unpeel the skin
      of ideology
and bring the core of urgency to the fore, unadorned, unattributed

For those who contact the coalition partners, photocopy, phone tree,
      mass mail,
e-post, tweet, disseminate, wheat paste, rain down w/o helicopter's aid

This is a poem for those who stand on street corners and gather
      signatures
who go door-to-door confronting the unknown, beguiling indifference
      or hostility

For those who fold the chairs after the planning meeting, gather the
      leftovers
(even the potato salad[11]), mop the floors, leave the room as it was
      found, close the lights

This is a poem for the one who, after booking the bus for the March
      on Washington
and finding (floor) space for folks in Logan Circle, closed his
      apartment door

And stood flattened by the desert gale of his need, yearned only for a
      man's arms
around him, the caress of beard against lips and the scruff of heart.

------

11   *reconfiguring itself now in the fluorescence*

With only the street lamp as illumination,
parka in a pool at his feet,

this poem is for him.

The Panther and the Bear

His inquiries had the touch of unrehearsed probing,
sparkling with interest.
His suggestions at association meetings were always sensible,
even eminently so,
delivered with curiosity and understatement:
Had we thought of this? We might want to consider …

The striations of his forearms rippled in discrete glory
and yet in seemingly choreographed unison—
this I noted with mesmerized gluttony,
as I held the door open for him,
on his return home from a bike ride
through the gathering of one August night.

Once, on the train,
he told me of his classes in a boxing gym,
and I imagined pirouettes graceful
and blows landed with force and accuracy
to the chagrin of his anonymous demons.

*(And yet the resident below complains of his ruckus,
several times even calling the police.
And how I marvel at the Rashomon-like chasm in our interpretations,
at her portrait of him: loud, loutish, lumbering.
As if instead of a panther above,
a bear was forever reaching for a honeycomb just out of reach.)*

Strange, then,
to exist with such intimate knowledge and yet without intimacy of
            any kind,
to live just a few feet away and to be forever apart.
Banter exchanged in the hallway all these many years, you see,
and no bread broken together,
no goblets raised in unison,
no veil removed from invitation,

and even when I was locked out of my apartment,
even when he stood with me in the lobby
as we waited for the locksmith, even then,
no entrée granted to sanctum ground.

1-866-Identity-Theft

Hello? Hello?
Who is this?
It's that same number,
howling in cellular triumph.
What is the root of your insistence?
I don't want to buy anything;
My funds are all tied up.
Bound and gagged, in fact.

Are you there?
How did you find me?
What list am I on? Who reported me?
Who discovered the chink in my bulletproof vest,
the hole in which to drill incessantly these misaligned digits?
Who exposed my privates to the data miner?
I only want to crouch here in the dark.
Help me find my pajama bottoms.
Please hurry.

Why is this happening?
What have I done?
By that I mean, what precisely?
How can I get you to stop calling?
How can I stop this ringing in my ear?
Can someone help me reach the operator?
Are there still operators?
How will I finish reconfiguring my portfolio?
Should I bother with this retirement plan?
Will it even matter?
I know I sent in my payment … didn't I?
Didn't I?
Hello? Hello? Hello?

Song For the Unknown Song

Remember that song?
The one then on every tongue and fingertip,
the one we heard in the car in San Francisco.
Granted, I was susceptible;
it was my first pilgrimage to the Holy City.
Remember how the movement sprawled outwards,
encountering trill and thrill and arpeggio
strategically placed for tingle?
And yet the violin chords anchored us,
gathered us in the city's embrace.
I loved seeing the hills and the cupolas
and the ocean and the balustrades
through your eyes.
How wide and welcoming everything became,
as if the panorama was framed by veranda curtains stirred by summer
        breezes.
The precision of your knowledge guided me to the beyond,
to the byways, alleys, lookouts,
even to Harvey's camera shop.
And all this long before the movie came out.
Everything I had heard so much about was somehow,
upon viewing, still so unexpected,
vibrating in a seventies Technicolor pointillist wash
as the song rippled through me,
as your hand,
massive, matted,
caressed my opening thighs,
with such certainty of movement
(*that surely had to reflect a certainty of intent*),
as the landmarks of liberation floated by,
as my foot tapped along with the percussionist's climb towards
        crescendo,
as I come upon this cable car curio in my night table drawer,
the (almost) only memento of that trip and time,
that trippy time.
If only I could remember that song!

Invocation

Come back to me.
Come back to me when the underworld lights blink in irregularity,
when the watering holes offer saccharine ale at a discount,
when the pounding of the dance hall leaves you only faintly curious.

Come back to me.
Come back to me when the swell of alien buttock barely distracts,
when the return of subway gaze sets a bounce in your step,
when the waiter's wink leads only to a round of Sunday brunch
      chuckles.

Come back to me.
Come back to me when words, cautiously suggested, can ring on
      soapstone,
when images screened in the dark lead to wonder, however measured,
      at dawn,
when face upturned finds refuge, however temporary, from nuclear
      rain.

I will be here still, here on the highest mountain top,
here where wolves howl at the sun,
here where poplars glimmer a path for the errant.
A plate will be set, a candle ablaze, arms will be ajar.

Come back to me. Come back to me.

Reunion Romp (A Costume Fantasy In Three Acts)

For Rav Sheftel Neuberger

Under the melancholy eye of the *neyr tomed*[12],
the lions tense nearby,
we youth, wiser now,
languidly absorb and share the swirling scents
only imagined long ago—
just to chill.
Levi Yitskhok, he warbles on King David and dew "laden" harps and
something else about willow trees.
So gentle, that one. Glibly, I'd forgotten.
Uri Tsvi, his cheekbones sculpted in the rumored despair
of Gaza revolutionaries,
conjures the Friday afternoon pilgrimages
to the mall where we (he) yearned for
Chrissie Hynde[13]
but went home with one clearly defined scoop of chopped liver.
He of the celebrated free fists (Menakhem Mendl),
only in recent years wielded against
other, less effeminate opportunities, listens and waits.
Through the cinnamon haze,
the fathers who staggered through these corridors and the alleys of
Vilna,
are invoked with reverence, with boredom.
My contribution: the relationship of the rooster to the aging *esreg*[14]
borrowed from the gentile who needs to be saved,
all this to the suddenly rapt scholars (it's in their blood),
whose voices slowly climb, languages multipy,
contentions narrow into a supple ferocity.

---

12 *neyr tomed (Yiddish, of Hebrew origin): the eternal light that hangs
above the ark in every synagogue as a symbol of God's eternal and immanent
presence*
13 *Chrissie Hynde (1951-), lead singer of the rock band The Pretenders*
14 *esreg (Yiddish, of Hebrew origin): citron, a fruit over which blessings are
recited during the Sukkot holiday*

Surveying my work, I clasp together my limp wrists,
toss my side curls and
laugh and laugh:
shive[15] over,
big pink beads all crazy-twisted,
this queen has returned to rule.

---

15   shive (Yiddish, of Hebrew origin): seven days of mourning after the death
of a close relative

Idyll

Cherish this banality, my love—
the day unfurling into splendor.
Coffee from below drifts into our reading lairs;
a lawn mower hums in the distance,
earth and words intoxicating us from dream.
Your footsteps patter down the corridor;
your night clothes gleam where the sun does not pierce,
a vision so fleeting yet glimpsed these countless times.
Today I won't rise to catch it.
I'll know you're there simply by the measure of my reverie,
carved in calm,
unmoved by the neighbor dog's yapping.
The weekend section spreads amply around the dining room table,
marked by circles of varying urgency.
Perhaps we will forage for treasure abandoned;
perhaps we will sample the fruit of vineyards coaxed into perfection.
Before we go to wherever we go,
I want to lift your hair, nuzzle your nape,
whisper my tender grateful nothings:
whatever these hours shall hold,
this is good, this is plenty.

III

Children

Danse Vivante

I was a gay fetus!
Paddling in Mama's waterways,
already awash in sticky fluid,
I craved cock.
When the hunky gyno started checking Mama out—
lifting here, poking there—
I got excited.
I couldn't help it. Oh, stop it!
The Reverend Jerry F. *olevasholem*[16]
peered at my sashaying form
on the sonogram and started gesticulating, shouting.
Hey, how did that guy get in here anyway?
Well, good thing the nurse was there to escort him out.
Contemplating her exiting form,
some ideas for jazzing up her uniform came to me:
a line here, a tuck there. Simple stuff really.
Early Project Runway kind of thing.
Postmodern "Lady with the Lamp"
piercing the era of prejudice
would be the title of her new look, I decided.
After the Rev.'s departure,
a Log Cabin Republican "accidentally" peeked in,
shuddered, and quickly excused himself.
With all the bouquets flooding in,
I kept concocting new arrangements.
Little busybody! Sit still. Behave!
When Gloria Gaynor was played in Muzak on the
p.a. system, I knew my time had finally come.
I plopped out between Mama's widespread legs
on to a float of lavender and white flowers—
carnations, irises, lilies, whatever I could throw together—
and efficiently cut the chord (snap snap snap!)
to the applause of the nurses and to Mama's eternal horror.

---

16 *olevasholem (Yiddish, of Hebrew origin): may he rest in peace*

Electroshock Cream Puff

Fuschia daisies leap from chamomile steppes.
Wolves in crinoline petticoats snuggle in Turkish-carpeted caves.

Plum tulips head-dance around the Parliament steps.
Coyotes sip rose water tea from gold rimmed jade goblets.

Irises remain stalwart under a blizzard of bon-bons,
even as jackals lap at reservoirs of newly discovered turquoise Tang.

The bulimic girl places a garland of hibiscus around her vomit pail,
while foxes band together and snarl the hounds at bay.

Please wait for me.
Don't go, Mother. I'm almost there.

Mythic Origins

Fun vanen kumt dayn loshn?
flegt men mikh fregn.
Where does your language come from?
They used to ask me.

I tried to retrace my steps
to locate the route of the sugar-free rock candy
winking in the thicket,
the footpath to the moment of original knowing.

I groped for narratives epic and narrow:
vistas of mass migration, societal upheaval,
(Great-Aunt Ettie vomiting overboard the creaking vessel),
demographics, tenements, dispersal to the outer rim,
but also the tempo of domestic discipline—
Father foraging through the weekly Torah portion,
Grandmother recounting the ingredients of ancient apple crisp
        delight.

I pontificated in tones I imagined to be "measured" on
words possessed, forgotten, regained.
Throughout, I aimed for phrases readily understood,
but still vivid, with a personal jolt.
I did it all. Really.
But understand this:
no one was convinced.

So now I no longer dissemble;
I recount a myth-in-progress, steeped in the fabulous.

I speak to you of groves, leafy and light-speckled,
where I wander about, unshackled by critique or concern.
My prancing through peach orchards is welcomed by nightingale
        choirs.

Here, my grammar is without mistake.
Well, still some, to be sure, but no one minds.
The broken glass of wrongly placed preposition,
the thorns of adjectival dis/agreements glitter yet in satanic pursuit.
I can't avoid them, you see, but strangely their daggers draw no blood.

The waves of my beloved's beard tickle my naked limbs;
his lips never tire of my form that he insists on calling "pearly,"
much to my mockery and delight.
His furry mass envelopes me,
as he too forages, like Father,
only for redemption of a different kind,
without restraint or shame.

Arms supple around me,
tendrils of hair escaped from her kerchief,
zingt di mame in oyer arayn
lider fun andere gan-eyden-steshkes/
Mother here sings in my ear
lyrics of other paradise lanes,
her voice unravaged by disease and longing.

Threshold Of Revolution: Volozhin[17], 1888

Despite the suggestion of sun,
the purple prose,
much is laid bare.
The splintery benches,
when no hosts could be found,
(*hakhnoses orkhim*[18] strategically invoked).
Even then, the stares,
curious, pitying. Amidst the ashen faces,
something not quite right about these explicit lips,
the spidery hands and the way they travel so slow,
so often.
Here, in the labyrinth of the warned,
the networks of the averted eye,
this gaze is all wrong,
ruined by the misplacement of its focus,
the abruptness of its departure.
The body gaunt like the others, yes,
but somehow flowing. As if on its way,
as if already there.
And the allure of the night waltzes with
the disciples of Reb Hayyim's heirs,
his breathtaking steps,
long tarnished by glimmers not yet clear,
having to do with lost realism and methodologies rediscovered
and bold banners.
All of this he somehow sees through the frost of the early morning
        panes,
written,
as he caresses his *tefillin*[19],
pausing on a favorite, well-worn zone,
knowing this will be the last time.

---

17 *Volozhin (now Valozhyn, Belarus): site of yeshiva renowned for its intensive
in-depth Talmudic study, founded by Reb Hayyim Volozhiner (1749-1821) in
1803 and closed in 1892*
18 *hakhnoses orkhim (Yiddish, of Hebrew origin): hospitality*
19 *tefillin: phylacteries*

Blossom

As the sun stretched its legs around him,
he found that he too could make himself comfortable,
or at least aim for a scrap of snooze.

He could disarm the terror in Mother's final clutching.
He could erase the image of trickster Father
unable to meet his eye,
his flight to prank and magic and fancy clipped at last.
No rabbits or cards or ivory tipped canes that night;
they would not fit into the allotted luggage.
He could subdue the drone of the announcement,
with its recitation of names and hush and
confusion and pleading and enormity.

The faded animal smells felt so reassuring against
his still crisp herringbone wool suit,
as he remembered outings to the mountains,
and the swarms of goats nuzzling his hand with the ticklish tongue
of their acceptance and the country lady explaining their ways.
Not so very long ago, either,
all of that.
He bit into the rolls that Mother had packed
and was surprised by their freshness.
He realized he was losing track of time, the order of things.

He thought about his old pals. The gang.
Greta, who almost never spoke,
but whom he could always understand.
Didi, with his frog collection, his damp breath,
his habit of breaking suddenly into cartwheels.
Until they were no longer permitted to come,
until they stopped coming.
Until he had to leave school entirely,
until some big boys forced him to pull down his pants
and beat him there,
until he slipped into a fog of dread without end.

Imagine his surprise, then, when tonight,
after he had removed his clothes,
folding them on the hay, he looked down
and saw that a foreskin had spontaneously sprouted!
He touched himself, to be sure, and yes, it really was true.
But it's impossible, he kept whispering and rocking,
it's impossible, it's impossible. Whispering and rocking.
Only a mouse, equally unsettled, witnessed his insistence.

Friday Afternoon Circle Play

The children don't know what to make of the spinster uncle,
how to interpret the negative space around his muscular frame.
In their confusion they articulate the unspeakable;
they voice the questions that hover nervously everywhere.

With creased brow they dig for origins and evolutions;
they don't understand how this man in seemingly good health
has traveled to them alone, devoid of spouse, devoid of brood,
simply (de)void. How is this so? When will it change?

Their mother, jogging between the hallah smoking in the oven,
the gefilte fish still too damp, and the soon-to-arrive Sabbath guests,
allows the interrogation to continue, uneasily, out of distraction,
but curious too about where it will all lead.

The children rise to encircle the spinster uncle in dance,
leaving him alone in the neon center.
They frame their questions anew in chant, which becomes accusation,
then declaration: "*Feter iz a goy! Feter iz a goy!*[20]"

Incredulous themselves over the coining of their new credo,
but eager for more interactive amusement,
the children scatter to various crevices and caves of the house.
The mother offers the spinster uncle some sponge cake.

Still rooted in the spotlight, he accepts her offering.
When she brings it to him, he mumbles his thanks,
but feeds it instead to the stuffed lion, bear, and monkey,
who have edged closer to form a circle of solace.

---

20 *Feter iz a goy! (Yiddish): Uncle isn't Jewish!*

Rub a Dub-Dub: Three Figures and a Tub

My sister-in-law kneels over the tub,
exhausted but relaxed in the evening steam.

Even in this position, her dress extends below her knees.
Her sleeves are rolled up, but not above the elbow.

She asks me to remind her of the *lokshn kugl*[21] in the oven,
of the dry cleaning that needs to be retrieved.

Not that she would forget these things.
But a little reminder can't hurt, she giggles.

You probably shouldn't be in here, she whispers suddenly.
But I won't tell anyone. You can stay.

I wink at her, knowing she won't see,
so immersed is she in the baby splashing away.

Where's baby going, she asks.
Show Uncle your duckie, she coos.

I squat to marvel at the toy
and the baby's chubby strawberry cream perfection.

Dangerously close to her mother, I nuzzle baby's neck,
feeling the happiness surging in her, the water prancing all around.

I stay down with her, seeking to trace the arcs of her gurgling,
swatting away at the need, once thought dormant, that she has
      unleashed.

---

21 *lokshn kugl (Yiddish): noodle pudding or loaf*

To My Niece, On Her Wedding

It has been so many years since I held you so close, so breathtaking,
so many years since I first beheld you: the firstborn, a miracle.

It has been so many years since the photo of you and your brothers,
the one that has stood next to my socks through the rupture(s), these
       many years.

It has been so many years since we played together, when our fancy
could fly unchecked in the realm of dolls and obedient husbands.

It has been so many years since we could draw together,
samplers of piety sketched over water taffy and Chinese noodles.

Just as I did with your mother, just as vivid in her vision,
just as precise in her rendering, so many years, nearly a generation
       earlier.

It has been so many years since I learned of your work,
the lilt of your years, the changing shades of your voice.

And here you are now, (as if) suddenly a woman, pulling out a chair,
laughing, making welcome, again like your mother.

Soon you will be in the arms of another. His will be the voice you hear
       in the dark.
The strands of his life will be braided with yours.

May you revere that twilight when we sampled 11 flavors at the
       turnpike's nape.
May you learn to decipher opaque tones. May your love flourish in
       deliberation.

Tonight, through the garlanded partition, on my raft perched atop
        waves of fedora,
I marvel at you, this you, so resplendent, the panorama of your
        radiance.

I send you these benedictions in secret, in remembrance of our
        together games,
and without ado, in honor of the new ones that await you with others.

Eros, Thanatos

Y., *in memoriam*

Even in death,
you remain in shadow,
cannot be named.
When others pronounce upon the new generation
coming up on *Will & Grace*,
free(er) of trauma,
I consider the resilience of the irrational, bigotry's will to endure
and my vow to not politicize your life and its end.
I think of you,

of our conversation on the August park bench
and your craving consuming uncontainable
and my fear and wanting so to shield you from danger
since you were only sixteen but looked much older
and had already had a go at self-annihilation.
There's plenty of time for that,
I groped, aiming for sensible tones, like a guidance counselor,
but succeeding only in clumsiness:
start small, get a degree and your own place, that's how I got out, you can
*   do this*

when all you sought was the shade of the lingering gaze, a confetti of
        kisses
and then there was your phone call or two
and then the move to a yeshiva in Switzerland of all places
and then nothing
until I heard the news, a conversational aside really,
and comprehension failed, could not forge a path to realization.
How could it be, it couldn't be: you,
discovered dead at nineteen of an overdose in a Miami Beach hotel
        room,
as if this were a B noir film, or a segment of *48 Hours*,

but it really was you, you, whom my sister-in-law,
anchored in tradition and your shared community,
tried so hard to save, you,
whom I, in my exile,
tried to affect from afar,
tried to point to other options,
but didn't stay, didn't follow up,
never realizing I wouldn't have the time to get it right.
You eluded us both. You eluded us all.

Forgive me, forgive me.

Reprise

Sometimes in the gym fighting gravity's march
under fluorescent candor I spot yet another white chest hair
sprouting seemingly in mid-sprout having dodged my pluck
not gray but white without metaphor
I try not to view this as foreshadowing
of a future without transition
of a plummeting directly into decrepitude

and I remember how nearly thirty years earlier I looked into other
glass and observed brown hair bursting forth sweeping the
expanse of torso and limbs
the pallor of me sullied forever by these marauders of night
how I would tug sobbing to no avail
no match were my tweezers and fingers for these forces
how quick and far-ranging were their cavalries no need had they for
         strategy or finesse

how I used to wonder if these hairs with their whorls and curlicues
their elaborate flourishes were themselves
like the snowflakes we had learned about grades so many grades before
each one unique never to be duplicated impossible to replace
only these were never to be displayed in paper interpretation on the
         school window
even though once Levi with a wink removed one from his chest and
placed it under a microscope much to the fury of our science teacher

and oh how I marveled at his curiosity and dispassion
his engagement with the self as object of scientific interest
and the fine form from which the strand had been so coolly taken
and wonder where Levi is now
having heard rumors of Southern California
and a car mechanic's garage and
sometimes wonder too about the current state of his chest

before returning to the present reality of my own
then back to Levi again to his play
his gift with numbers and equations his patient
largely unsuccessful attempts at rendering their elegance visible to me
and wish so I could bring him to me
to be with him close tight to be even just once again
all asparkle in the embrace of his conspiratorial wink

Without, Within

Having failed to "be fruitful and multiply"
remaining without fruit (but still fruity)
without woman (or man, for that matter)
and without child behold the dawning of smile
the forms of movement the miracle of creation and change
that he witnesses in visits to family
where he sits stark an embodiment of absence
a harbinger of desert a vast sandstorm-scape of sorts
but also an exemplar of frolic and glee
the reluctantly conferred role of the maiden uncle
permitted even here as he plays with the children
hiding behind the giant stuffed giraffe
serving tea to the girls and the lady panda
blowing rainbow bubbles to baby
exulting in her rapture
and yes even building forts for the newly militarized zone
GI Joe is endlessly inventive he observes in wonder
how supple he is here in a way he can never be
outside the playroom's stone walls
where he dances turning tripping avoiding
sometimes forgetting which topic is forbidden
which reference to omit which to foreground
how to stay in synch with the contours of his yarmulke
which despite its soup bowl shape keeps almost falling off
that piece of cloth at once familiar and foreign
trying to be if not the model uncle
then at least some sort of uncle visible if noticed
though (apparently) unable to create another branch
or compare notes on childhood development
ever an onlooker a role forged in late childhood with its stirrings
never a contributor to life cycle landmarks
but still to be somehow a presence an option
to suggest really to discover renew a dignity in the quotidian
in support offered and received
words tried on and felt

exchanged grappled with over coffee committed to paper
deeds informed by knowledge and hopefully justice
extended to community and perhaps thereby planet
gestures steady small but perhaps not minor
refusing retreat into devastation that devil always hovering
and with niece's pudgy hand (still permitted) in his own
insisting on *doikayt*[22]
and a path however narrow along the byways of grace

---

22 *doikayt (Yiddish): hereness*

Boys' Night Out (The Missing Poem)

The charisma of the Saturday night kosher pizzeria has not waned.
Youth of both genders still come to mingle
in this de-militarized zone,
to explore the outer reaches of the permissible,
to test the elasticity of rabbinic injunction. To a point.

The classic ingredients—
oregano, tomato sauce, cheese, garlic, bravura—
flirt here with freshly minted hormones
molded by nearly ankle length skirts (a few of these in denim),
blouse sleeves hovering around the elbow
but still form-fitting (in some cases),
white shirts, yarmulkes, tsitses[23] and
the gyrations of synthesized Ortho-pop over the loudspeaker.

He sits with his nephews, two young men and a boy.
We'll have to call them *Alef*, *Beys*, and *Giml* for now, at a corner table.
Alef is slim, debonair, but also skeptical, brooding,
having drifted to the periphery of the yeshiva world.
Beys must surely be a heartthrob, the object of maidenly pining,
with a strapping build and eyes so blue.
The boy, *Giml*, is playful, savoring his slice, diddling with the
        toppings.

The talk moves effortlessly.
He learns of *Alef*'s part-time work at a men's clothing store.
Beys tells of his new yeshiva, his roommate,
even the Talmudic section he's now studying.
Giml is excited about beginning Talmud study
and those darn (New York) Yankees—
the only blot on the conversation!

---

23   tsitses (Yiddish, of Hebrew origin): *four-cornered fringed garment worn
by observant Jewish males*

As the words curve and careen,
he becomes light-headed, refusing to grope for steady ground.
A sense of well-being, amidst the uncertainty, envelopes him.
This once, he doesn't think about his departure or inadequacy.
Still, he can't quite believe this is happening. Perhaps it isn't?
Might this always have been?
Their mother, his sister, stands at the door, beaming.

IV

Strangers At Your Gate

Nostalgia

In the city of my birth,
a calm pervaded the millinery.
Black was the choice of men;
women wore gray everywhere.
White was seen not as variety, but as completion.

In the city of my birth,
no one could get lost.
Streets were as clear as the first geometry lesson;
visitors soon discarded their maps.
This was what our first fathers had intended.

In the city of my birth,
the curls of wigs stiffened; a second chin quivered.
In late night alleys hooded figures hurried to and fro.
In the morning it was clear that the upcoming years would not be
        easy.
This was how we understood revolution.

In our city people came to breathe deep.
They found in our halls a space to contemplate anew.
Here voices from above spoke in mild refrain.
Even the bullies paused under the sweep of our renowned arches.
Our name spread far and wide.

In the city of my birth,
strife was not unknown, but not encouraged.
Even the dogs understood this.
Many have speculated on our formula. Entirely to no avail.
Our love was called brotherly.

However there were those who were seduced by other cities,
drawn by brighter color, a more varied music.
We imagined we could simply transplant the legacy of our city
and that our role of emissary would be welcomed.
But the city of our birth refused to release its secrets.

94

We always praised the city of our birth.
We spoke of all that it had bequeathed us, never of ourselves as
        thieves.
Only in the moments before sleep did we sometimes
remember the final closing of the city gates behind us,
the intimate fury of their slam.

בענקשאַפֿט

אין מײַן היימשטאָט
האָט אַ רו באַהערשט די פּוצערײַ.
שװאַרץ האָבן די מענער אויסגעקליבן;
די פֿרויען שטענדיק אין גרוי.
װאָס איז געװען בײַ אונדז נישט קיין װאַריאַנט, נאָר אַ מין גאַנצקייט.

אין מײַן היימשטאָט
האָט מען פֿאַרבלאָנדזשען נישט געקאָנט.
די גאַסן זײַנען געװען קלאָר װי אַן ערשטע געאָמעטריע־לעקציע;
די געסט האָבן זיך אַװעקגעװאָרפֿן זייערע מאַפּעס.
אַזוי איז געװען די כּוונה פֿון אונדזערע אָבֿות.

אין מײַן היימשטאָט
זײַנען די שײטל־לאָקן שטײַף געװאָרן; אַ גױדער האָט געציטערט.
אין שפּעט־נאַקטיקע געסלעך זײַנען באַקאַפּטערטע פֿיגורן געלאָפֿן אַהין און צוריק.
אין דער פֿרי איז קלאָר געװאָרן אַז די צוקונפֿט װעט נישט זײַן גרינג.
אַזוי האָבן מיר פֿאַרשטאַנען רעװאָלוציע.

אין אונדזער היימשטאָט זײַנען מענטשן געקומען אַטעמען טיף.
זיי האָבן געפֿונען אין אונדזערע זאַלן װו צו קלערן אויף ס׳נײַ.
דאָ האָבן קולער פֿון אויבן גערעדט אין אַ מילדן רעפֿראַן.
אַפֿילו די בריטאַנעס האָבן זיך אָפּגעשטעלט אונטערן פֿאַרנעם פֿון אונדזערע
באַרימטע בויגנס.
אונדזער שם האָט זיך פֿאַרשפּרייט.

אין מײַן היימשטאָט
האָט מען יאָ געװוּסט פֿון מחלוקת אָבער מע האָט עס נישט געמוטיקט.
אַפֿילו די הינט האָבן דאָס פֿאַרשטאַנען.
אַ סך מענטשן האָבן זיך פֿאַרטראַכט װעגן אונדזער פֿאַרמל. אָבער אומזיסט.
אונדזער ליבשאַפֿט האָט מען אָנגערופֿן ברידערלעך.

96

אָבער ס'זײַנען געווען די וואָס זײַנען פֿאַרפֿירט געווארָן פֿון אנדערע שטעט,
צוגעצויגן צו העלערע פֿאַרבן, א וואַריִיִרטער מוזיק.
מיר האָבן געמיינט אַז מיר קענען איבערפֿלאַנצן די ירושה פֿון דער שטאָט.
און אַז מע וועט וואַרעם אויפֿנעמען אונדזער ראָלע פֿון שליח.
אָבער אונדזער היימשטאָט האָט זיך אָפגעזאָגט אויסצוזאָגן אירע סודות.

מיר האָבן שטענדיק געלויבט אונדזער היימשטאָט.
מיר האָבן גערעדט וועגן אַלץ וואָס זי האָט אונדז געגעבן בירושה,
אָבער קיין מאָל נישט וועגן זיך אַליין ווי גנבֿים. נאָר האַרט פֿארן שלאָפֿן גיין
האָבן מיר א מאָל זיך דערמאָנט אין דעם לעצטן פֿאַרמאַכן פֿון די שטאָטטויערן,
דעם אינטימען כּעס פֿון זייער פֿאַרהאַקן זיך.

Landscape: Obscured, Silver

What has come of the ghosts who once dwelt among us?
Flitting between our bent shoulders,
they ensured that our involvement was understood.
Their wreaths shielded us from
the black grains that dotted our fields of surrender.
With their hands caressing our back,
the snow glittered on the expanse of our pilgrimage.
With or even without lanterns,
our feet could remap the inevitable road—
the sluices of brown, the dog bite against our ankles, the gathering
       wind.
This was a world whose name eluded us,
ruled by an earth furious at our invasion
and by a heavens insistent on exile.
Who then were these intermediary creatures?
What was the terrain of their intention?
Spurred by fear, we welcomed their intervention.
Such a grace could only enlarge.
Surely our strength was not a mistake?!
We had trudged these hundreds of miles;
each step had to have been a triumph.
We had arrived; we knew it.
These were our rooms.
Outside—our gardens.
What then this darkness?
Why had our words become so pale,
our fingers so gossamer?

לאנדשאפֿט: פֿאַרטונקלט, זילבער

וואָס איז געוואָרן פֿון די רוחות וואָס האָבן אַ מאָל געלעבט צווישן אונדז?
לויפֿנדיק צווישן אונדזערע אײַנגעבויגענע פּלייצעס, אַהין און אַהער,
האָבן זיי געגעבן דעם עולם צו פֿאַרשטיין אונדזער באַטייליקונג.
זייערע קרעגץ האָבן אונדז באַשיצט פֿון
די שוואַרצע קערלעך וואָס האָבן באַפֿינטלט די פֿעלדער פֿון אונדזער
קאַפּיטוליירונג.
מיט די הענט זייערע וואָס האָבן געגלעטט אונדזערע רוקנס,
האָט דער שניי געגלאַנצט איבערן אויסשפּרייט פֿון אונדזער נסיעה.
מיט אָדער אַפֿילו אָן לאַמטערנס,
האָבן אונדזערע פֿיס געקענט ווידעראַמפּעווען דעם באַשערטן וועג —
די ברוינע שליוזן, דעם הונטביס לעבן אונדזערע קנעבלעך, אַ וואָקסנדיקער ווינט.
דאָס איז אַ וועלט וואָס מיר האָבן נישט געקענט באַנאָמענען,
באַהערשט פֿון אַן ערד מלא כעס איבער אונדזער אינעוואייזיע
און פֿון אַ הימל וואָס האָט זיך אײַנגעשפּאַרט אז מיר מוזן זײַן אין גלות.
ווער זײַנען געווען אָט די צווישנדיקע בריאות?
וואָס איז געווען דער באָדן פֿון זייער כּוונה?
געטריבן פֿון מורא, האָבן מיר זיי באַגריסט.
אזאַ הן האָט נאָר געקענט פֿאַרגרעסערן.
אונדזער כּוח איז זיכער נישט געווען קיין טעות!?
מיר האָבן זיך געשלעפּט הונדערטער מײַלן;
יעדער טראָט האָט געמוזט זײַן אַ נצחון.
מיר זײַנען אָנגעקומען; דאָס האָבן מיר געוווסט.
דאָ זײַנען אונדזערע צימערן.
אין דרויסן — אונדזערע גערטנער.
איז צו וואָס אזאַ חושך?
פֿאַר וואָס זײַנען אונדזערע ווערטער אזוי בלייך געוואָרן
און אונדזערע פֿינגער ווי ארץ־ישראל־פֿעדעם?

99

Paradox

This land, too, is holy,
although no families have been truncated over its charms,
no empires have crumbled over its indecipherable shapes,
no young man's life has ebbed away over its occasional fronds.

This land, too, is holy,
although no orange blossoms have rained down in random grace,
no plums have stained it with refreshment,
no almonds have been born of its clenched womb.

This land, too, is holy,
although no endangered animals have sought its jagged embrace,
no protests have been mounted over its vast lack,
no legislation has been enacted to protect it from its own absence.

This land, too, is holy.
Shunned, reviled, cursed,
it unfolds for miles beneath wind and rain.
It gleams in abandon. Its desolation refuses ode and elegy.

Squirrels! (On the Eve Of the Pogrom)

There they are, those rodents of the sun—
catapulting their gray, brown, drab existence,
a mélange of furtiveness and defiance,
into the reverie of day.

Look at the bushy, no, frizzy tails—ever gesticulating,
overheated, overexcited, over … emoting.
The click and clack of their argumentation,
the din of their jabber,
as if they were the only ones in the yard or the park.
As if they were the only ones here,
as if they had never heard of the word "modulated."
Have they no respect? No sense of propriety?
Don't they know things are not done this way?
It just isn't decent.

Then, as if their own internal squabbles were not enough,
they try to lure others into their devious byways,
stirring up trouble,
rounding up other malcontents,
suckling on the woes of the vulnerable or the unsuspecting.
Bloodsuckers! Parasites!

And the way they hoard foodstuff,
stealing from the paws of diligent animals,
toying with the market supply of acorns and nuts,
all for greed and power.
Things were so much better before they got here.
There was a time when they weren't here, wasn't there?
Don't you remember that lovely era now bygone?

Let's not forget the matter of their teeth, either.
Why just the other day, they gnawed through
my newly installed eaves. Can you believe it?
Why me? How did they zero in on my roof?
It's those beady eyes, of that there can be no doubt.

Nothing can be shielded from their laser-like glare.
With those eyes and those teeth,
it won't be long before our way of life is destroyed.

If only they really were mice—
meek, confined to the walls and the outskirts of things,
with occasional nocturnal forays,
grateful for our crumbs—
then we could handle them!
Even our cats, bred for efficiency, have proven ineffective.
We'll have to notify the local authorities to take this on,
or perhaps even the feds.
This matter cannot be left to fester.
Our living space has become infested.
We have been overrun. We cannot breathe.
How can we go on like this?
What choice do we have?
We must reclaim our land!

Jewish Spring

Winter birds brush our faces in farewell.
Our step quickens as thaw gains force and marches into inevitability.
Flowers, bold in their delicacy,
viewed since time's beginning,
are seen anew, interpreted afresh.
Everyone sees flowers in a different way, Rinah once said.
Trees spread cover thickly
between the chemical groves below and above,
insisting on their leafy say.
Hands pool the earth, laying the foundation for renewal.
Already we envision stalks bent with bounty.
We breathe these many fragrances, humbled, awed.
But like the gazelle on the savannah,
our eyes are always shielded toward the horizon.
We peruse the headlines and the top stories;
we assess the pitch of the chatter.
Who knows how long this generosity,
how deep this permissibility.
Dogwood blossoms etch our prayer in grace.

Silence = Life

After the ACT UP motto "Silence = Death"

The epithets were squashed.
The chat rooms were silent;
salons were now the order of the day.
The paraphernalia were displayed only in museum halls.
The tones on the wall placards reflected a curiosity in the historical;
all cautionary notes had been removed.
The posters and pamphlets were relegated to rare book reading rooms.
They were to be understood as emblems of a dusty weltanschauung.
Shaved heads were at last merely a fashion statement.
The anthems once beerily chanted were refashioned for the cabaret,
with sequins and panache.
Boots marching on cobblestones at midnight
inspired an unfamiliar sense of security.
The brass was removed;
the fists disassembled.
Stunned, we unbolted our shutters and warily peered out.
The winds in the town square had died down.
The garbage fluttered no more.
We were no longer despised.

Alternative Yuletide

No, this isn't what you think.
This won't be a poem for Jews for Jesus.

There won't be a dilution of symbols here,
nor a call to theological potpourri.

No, this won't be a Irving Berlin-ish revelry,
sparkling in sleigh bells and whiteness.

Instead, there will be gratitude for the day off,
for the streets so desolate, for the stores sealed,

There will be relief in freedom from obligation and the search for
        objects.
There will be contentment in apart-ness, in not looking in from the
        outside.

We will meet beneath the cinema's neon-rimmed crystal chandelier,
consider the various offerings, without hurry, and despite the queues,
        without stress.

Afterwards, we will trek downtown, no matter the weather,
where avenues narrow to alleys, where restaurant windows perspire in
        beckoning.

There we will discuss what we've seen,
savor the vigorous fare, envisioned across oceans, revised here.

We will toast this plenty—the fellowship,
the nourishment, the possibilities for renewal,

this mild delight, this muted reverence,
this holiday.

Wandering Jew In Little Rome

Brookland, Washington, D.C.

What forces marshaled imagined otherwise led to this landing?
Father has always pleaded with me to live among my people.
Who exactly are my people? Where do the borders of folk begin?
I've always wanted to ask him but never do.
Baedeker in hand ever the diligent traveler
I try to follow the guideposts to
mercy perpetual adoration immaculate
Claire sister Holy Cross national shrine
archdiocese bishops Jesuit Dominican
St. Francis Trinity Franciscan
the list ongoing
the many variables and varieties
that elude my grasp
and so I keep circling in my ignorance and torpor
until my guidebook dampens from confusion
stumbling unable to visualize the other side
and trying not to think of the Inquisition
the Expulsion from Spain and Portugal
and the policies on queer desire souls
my other people
and wondering what would happen to the world
if the Pope released an encyclical
declaring homosexuality sublime a gift divine
and how reckless it all seems to
burn these words onto screen and page
for fear still of the auto-da-fé
but taking caution
not to blunt the nuance
the spectrum of expression and voice
to honor the bounty of dissent
the refusal to leave quietly
Dorothy Day[24] Liberation Theology Dignity

---

24 *Dorothy Day (1897-1980), co-founder of the Catholic Worker movement*

until in the end this isn't a statement or
perhaps even a poem really
but a few lines for consideration
of judiciousness reached for but perhaps not attained
of late Sunday afternoon strolls along grace's promenade
staring at signs and symbols and landmarks undeciphered
but grateful always for this shelter these embers of light
and the pines and the ghosts flickering between them

Little Bird, Among the Monuments

Children, come closer the better to see.
This is the Uncle Feygele in his natural habitat.
Watch him move about his nest with ease.
With such care does he assemble
twigs and ribbons and ornithological bric-a-brac,
the concerto of his clutter.
How well he knows each surface and their
relationship to the structure as a whole!
Here he is at dawn chomping on raspberry-flecked granola.
You know how they love that stuff!
By "they" I mean those dun-colored birds
of an indeterminate urban variety.
Sparrows? Starlings? Wrens perhaps? How should I know?
Observe too how he flutters between
columns and pavilions and naked ladies and gents.
The tourists pay him no mind;
consider this therefore a seat
at a concert of the music, not of the sublime,
but of the quotidian.
Let there be no ruckus or even whispering among you,
lest you disturb the gauze of his nightfall.
Hush now, little ones.
For yes, here is he once more,
returned in elated exhaustion
from the refreshment of fountain water cooled by marble.
But with the eagles and the jaguars ever on the prowl,
he needs your attention and warning.
He depends on you, you know.
How odd it is to say that.
Although you can't see his repose, children,
understand that your vigilance is essential
to ensure the eminence of his ethereal domain.

Poem, Kicking and Screaming

I can't squeeze this feeling—
this darkness, these flakes of rust glittering in the Indian summer
        sun—
into a poem.
The blue vultures, circling overhead,
chant their eagerness and patience.
How is it that can I decipher their summons,
when homes are shuttered,
when there is no light in the piazza,
when sound itself has been outlawed.

Don't embark on any expeditions.
This is hardly the time to invoke the claims of archaeology.
The shovels are all corroded, in any case.
Don't be swayed by the seduction of the train,
the cadence of the iron wheels,
the swaying re-wind to the era before the caress was bungled.
Don't come with me into the tunnel,
Do not take me there where it's darker yet.

Lie here with me instead.
Help me locate the tapestry of blankness.
Through the mayhem of the Styrofoam peanut jitterbug,
read to me from words,
discovered on cave walls,
found on paper scraps fluttering in the bus shelter,
scrawled on napkins from the 24-hour Chinese take-out,
spray-painted on the underbelly of the interstate overpass.

Stay with me,
until dusk descends.
Stay with me,
until the comets begin their cautious approach.
Stay with me,
at least until then,
at least until I squeeze this feeling from the poem,
until I emerge with something unfettered,
until my ascent ensures the disarray of the blue vultures.

Thanksgiving

In dream I was called to the Torah
in sing-song was I there beckoned: *yaamoyd der alter bokher*[25] ...
my nephews were all around
my nieces too and not in the balcony either
and all of their little and not-so-little ones in holiday best
and I did not stumble and I did not blush
but surged forward
and this time I did not invoke the One
asher bahar banu mi-kol ha-amim/
who chose us from among all the nations
but instead gave thanks to this nation here
to the dawn light sifted by mountain birches
to the red oh so red flowers gushing from cactus prickle
and I did not agitate over the verses troubling
the ones on chosenness and the other about "abomination"
you know all about them so infamous are they
and in any case can be located easily enough
now that there's Google so no excuses
but neither did I circumvent them skittishly
and thus did I not instigate unease
nor approval but only appraisal
until my song was accompanied by those
who knew the melody all along
coursing somehow into togetherness hitherto unexperienced
until the borders of I expanded crumbled
until there was no longer an I but only we/us
not vague or diffuse or mystical
but altogether lithe and exhilarating
was this what Freud meant by "oceanic feeling"
only I had never been so blessed in my retreats
the meditations on the boulders aloof by the sea
so that others many others came to join us

---

25 *yaamoyd der alter bokher (mixture of Hebrew and Yiddish): Calling the
old bachelor*

and there were no longer questions on the brotherhood of nations
since there were no longer nations if only for this moment
nor were there disparaging charges of idealism and naïveté
but only a buoyancy and a lyric gladdening
and a proclamation of a golden age
uninterrupted by measured steps and pragmatism and awakening

Emerald Moon, In Broad Daylight

For Janine Medlin
(Leaving Connemara, 2008)

In this –scape, this land

    neither

        earth nor water

    rain nor sun   blue nor gray

    clear nor misty   cold nor warm

      but something entirely other

here in this land

    both

lush and foreboding   green and brown   rocky and boggy soft

    dense with riddle   and centuries of defiance

half-mad from jetlag and chilled bones

    I stumbled along the river bank

tripping over those stones renowned and my greed for mystical
    cleaving

when I heard a call from long ago

      misplaced, disregarded all these years,

an invitation to come forward into the circle of music and shadow

      I put down the souvenirs arrayed before me

the scarves the sweaters the marble the crystal all the gleaming things

      and listened   and shivered

and reached for hands extended in welcome

שמאָראַק־לבנה, אין מיטן העלן טאָג

דזשאַנין מעדלינען
(אויפֿן וועג פֿון קאַנעמאַראַ, 2008)

אין דעם —שאַפֿט, אָט דעם לאַנד

נישט

ערד נישט וואַסער

נישט רעגן נישט זון   נישט בלוי נישט גרוי

נישט קלאָר נישט נעפלדיק   נישט קאַלט נישט וואַרעם

אָבער עפּעס אין גאַנצן אַנדערש

דאָ אין אָט דעם לאַנד

סײ

גיביק סײ בייז׳סימנדיק   סײ גרין סײ ברוין   סײ שטיינערדיק סײ זומפּיק ווייך

געדיכט מיט רעטעניש   און יאָרהונדערטער פֿון צולהכעיתן

האַלב־משוגע פֿון דזשעטלעג און דורכגעקילטע ביינער

האָב איך געשטאַמפּערט בײַם ברעג פֿון טײַך

זיך סטאָפּיקעט אין יענע באַרימטע שטיינער און מײַן גיריקייט נאָך דבֿיקות

114

ווען איך האָב געהערט אן אויפֿרוף פֿון וואַיטן אמאָל

פֿאַרלייגט, פֿאַרקוקט אָט די אַלע יאָרן,

אַ פֿאַרבעטונג אַריַינצוקומען אינעם קריַיז פֿון מוזיק און שאַטן

איך האָב אַנידערגעלייגט די סוווענירן אויסגעלייגט פֿאַר מייַנע אויגן

די שאַלן סוועטערס מאַרמאָר קריסטאַל אַלע גלאַנצנדיקע זאכן

און האָב זיך צוגעהערט   און האָב געציטערט

און האָב געזוכט הענט אויסגעשטרעקט מיך אויפֿצונעממען

Notes

"Feygele" (pronounced: "fey" as in "Tina Fey," "ge" as in "get," and "le" as in "let"), derived from the Yiddish term פֿױגל, from the German *Vogel* (bird) and the Yiddish diminutive marker " –le," is a term meaning a man who is or is thought to be a homosexual. Although widely used in contemporary parlance, this meaning of the word is not given in Uriel Weinreich's *Modern English-Yiddish Yiddish-English Dictionary* where "feygele" is defined as "checkmark." Feygele is also the diminutive form of the Yiddish feminine name, Feyge. I relish too its proximity in sound to the words "fey" and "fag." Given its rich etymology and usage, I chose to use it in the collection's title, fully aware of the challenges it might pose to some readers.

Yiddish words and phrases in this book are transliterated according to the system established by the YIVO Institute for Jewish Research. For the sake of uniformity, I considered words and phrases of Hebrew origin accepted into Yiddish as Yiddish and transliterated them as such, although they might be familiar to more readers as Hebrew. Therefore, נר תמיד is transliterated as *neyr tomed* and not as *ner tamid*. Words accepted into English (i.e. Kaddish, tefillin, and yeshiva) follow the spelling of *Webster's Third New International Dictionary*.

Acknowledgments

I am grateful to the editors of the following publications in which these poems, sometimes in different form, first appeared or are scheduled to appear:

"Reunion Romp (a Costume Fantasy in Three Acts)," *Backspace*, Summer 1994; "Wandering Jew in Little Rome," *Beltway Poetry Quarterly*, Fall 2010; "Invocation," *Breadcrumb Scabs*, August 2009; "Cat Lady's Request" and "Walking with Sarina," *Dark Lady Poetry*, November 2009; "Friday Afternoon Circle Play," *Eclectica Magazine*, July/August 2010; "What Agnès Whispered," *Eudaimonia Poetry Review*, Summer 2010; "A Map of Commotion" (English and Yiddish), *Five Fingers Review*, 2002; "To the Poet, No Longer Young, Introverted by Nature," *Flutter Poetry Journal*, June 2009; "Jewish Spring" and "Landscape: Obscured, Silver" (English and Yiddish), *The Forward*, August 24, 2007 and April 25, 2003; "Voyeur's Diary," *Ganymede*, October 2010; "Bodies on Fire," *Koleinu: Our Voice*, June 1994; "Alternative Yuletide" and "Idyll," *Loch Raven Review*, Summer 2009; "Hebrew Lullaby" (English and Yiddish), *News of Yiddish Happenings in Los Angeles*, Winter/Spring 2004; "Border Crossing: Corridor, 7:35 p.m.," *Pemmican*, posted October 2009; "Emerald Moon, in Broad Daylight," "On Rejection: a Valentine," "Reprise," "Rub-a- Dub-Dub: Three Figures and a Tub," "Silence=Life," and "Smitten," *Praxilla*, posted October 25, 2009; "Remembering Rosa Luxemburg in the 'New' Times Square," *protestpoems.org*:, posted May 22, 2010; "The Last Music Lesson" and "To the Soldier, Sitting Opposite on the Riverdale Bound Train," *Queens College Journal of Jewish Studies*, Spring 2009; "Stories of Ida" and "Threshold of Revolution, Volozhin, 1888," *Response*, Winter/Spring 1996 and Summer 1995; "Paradox," *The South Carolina Review*, Fall 2009; "Instead of a Manifesto" (English and Yiddish) and "Nostalgia" (English and Yiddish), *Step by Step: Contemporary Yiddish Poetry/Trot bay trot: haynttsaytike Yidishe poezye* (Verbarium/Quodlibet, 2009); "Mythic Origins," *Stone's Throw Magazine*, Issue # 5, posted October 2010; "Instead of a Manifesto" (Yiddish), *Tsukunft*, April- September 2001; "The Blind Man in the Arms of the Prostitute," *Two Review*, 2011.

Gitl Schaechter-Viswanath proofread the Yiddish version of "Instead of a Manifesto" and "Nostalgia." Hershl Hartman proofread the Yiddish version of "Hebrew Lullaby." Sheva Zucker proofread all of the Yiddish that appears in the book with sensitivity and warmth. Their engagement with my work has strengthened it immeasurably. Roger Kohn provided French linguistic feedback on the title of the poem "Danse Vivante."

Aaron Mayer Frankel graciously permitted use of "Hasid Mask with Green Background" as the cover image of the book.

Yankl Salant typeset the Hebrew and Yiddish, proofread the Yiddish, and offered invaluable technical guidance as well as suggestions on the "Notes" page.

I am profoundly grateful to Susan Bright of Plain View Press for her unflagging support of this project.

As I send this book out into the world, I note some of the individuals who have made my words feel welcome. I give thanks to Angelika Bammer, Rivka Basman Ben-Haim, Andrew W.M. Beierle, Sholem Berger, Ann Brener, Regie Cabico, Mary Baine Campbell, Ellen Cassedy, Melissa Cook and Ken Giese, Peter Covino, Jim Feldman and Natalie Wexler, Krysia Fisher, Allen J. Frank and Faye-Ann Schott, Scott Free, Daniel Galay, Miriam Isaacs, Charles Jensen, Esther Kaplan, Mrs. Yaakov Klein, Julia Spicher Kasdorf, Dov-Ber Kerler, Cecile Kuznitz, Laura Levitt, Jeff Mann, Erin McGonigle, James Meyer, Christopher Murray, Peggy Pearlstein, Elzbieta Pelish, Jenny Price, T. Cole Rachel, Randall Reade, Eve Rifkah, Kim Roberts, Yankl Salant, Paul Edward Schaper, Jeffrey Shandler, Gregg Shapiro, Naomi Seidman, David Shneer, Myra Sklarew, Adele Steiner, Bernard Vaisbrot, Dan Vera, Sheva Zucker, and my sister, Rachel Berman.

Pearl Gluck has been a friend and a champion of my work for many years. I cherish and honor Pearl's artistic vision and her encouragement, counsel, and love.

This one's for you, baby.

About the Author

Yermiyahu Ahron Taub is the author of two previous volumes of poetry, *The Insatiable Psalm* (Hershey , PA, Wind River Press, 2005) and *What Stillness Illuminated/Vos shtilkayt hot baloykhtn* (West Lafayette , IN, Parlor Press, 2008; Free Verse Editions series). His English language poems have appeared in numerous publications, including *Beltway Poetry Quarterly*, *Eclectica Magazine*, *Flutter Poetry Journal*, *Free Verse*, *The South Carolina Review*, and *Stone's Throw Magazine*. His Yiddish language poems have appeared in such publications as *Der Bavebter Yid*, *Five Fingers Review*, *The Forward*, *Jews*, *Lilliput Review*, *Queer Poets Journal*, *Tsukunft*, and *Yugntruf*. He lives in Washington, D.C. Visit his web site at www.yataub.net.

Photo by Andrew W. M. Beierle

www.ingramcontent.com/pod-product-compliance
Lightning Source LLC
Chambersburg PA
CBHW071236020426
42333CB00015B/1495